Take a Look, It's in a Book

How Television Is Made at

Ronnie Krauss

Photographs by
Christopher Hornsby

Walker and Company
New York

Dear Reader,

I'm really glad you picked up this book. You're doing exactly what all of us at *Reading Rainbow* hope our viewers will do: you're *reading*! That's the whole reason we make our TV show—to turn kids like you on to good books and the joys of reading. So I'm thrilled to know that watching our show has led you to open a book.

When I was a child my mother was a teacher, and there were always books in our house. So I learned young, probably at about your age, that reading is like magic: It can take you anywhere in your imagination. And that's not only true when you're a kid—it lasts your whole lifetime. But—as you've heard me say a hundred times on the show— you don't have to take *my* word for it. Find out for yourself!

LeVar Burton

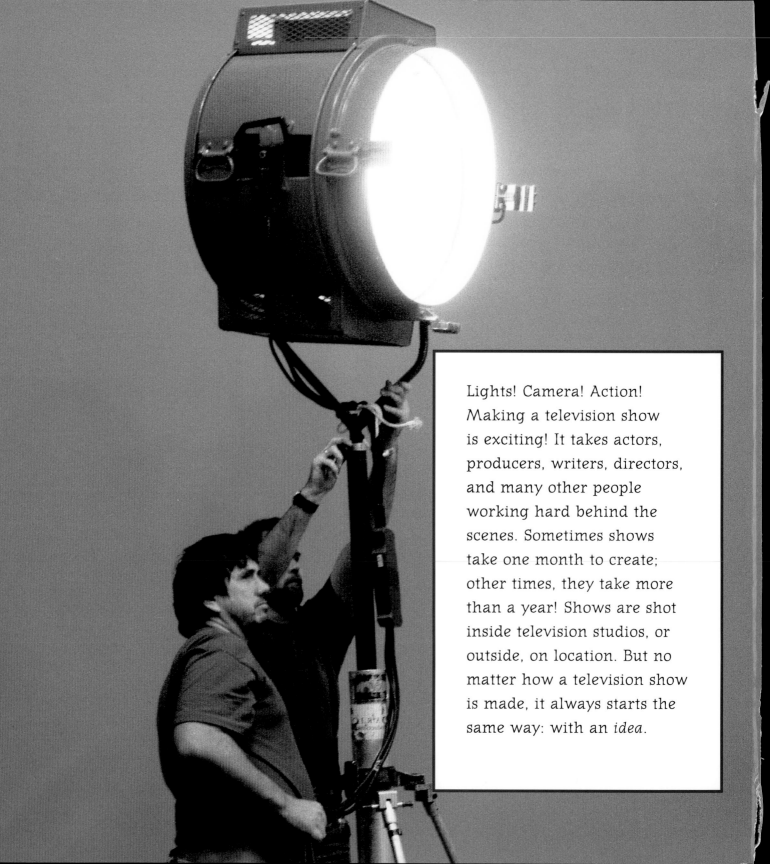

Lights! Camera! Action! Making a television show is exciting! It takes actors, producers, writers, directors, and many other people working hard behind the scenes. Sometimes shows take one month to create; other times, they take more than a year! Shows are shot inside television studios, or outside, on location. But no matter how a television show is made, it always starts the same way: with an *idea*.

The idea for every *Reading Rainbow* show comes from a great children's book. The rest of the show is built around the *theme*, or subject, of that book.

The staff at *Reading Rainbow* reads thousands of books every year. They pore over every page, asking questions about each book. Does it have an exciting story? Will the pictures look good on television? Is the story about a subject that can be explored in other ways? And finally, the most important question: Will children like the book?

Karen, the book manager, tests the books with children. Then Orly and Cecily, the supervising producers, and Twila, the executive producer, decide which books—out of everyone's favorites—will become *Reading Rainbow* shows. They pick only ten books a year.

Today they have chosen *Always My Dad*, the story of a family, to become a *Reading Rainbow* show.

Once a book is selected, the staff meets to plan the show. The book itself will appear as one *segment*, or part of the show, but there will also be other segments about the book's theme. The staff *brainstorms* ideas for these segments.

Brainstorming is hard work, but it can also be fun. Whenever an idea pops into someone's head, they just say it out loud—no matter how weird or silly it might seem. Sometimes the craziest ideas are the best!

Today everyone has suggestions. "*Always My Dad* is about a girl whose father lives far away," says Kathy, a producer. "So let's meet a real-life family like the one in the book." Mark, a director, remembers that there is a "Family Day" race in New York's Central Park in a few months, and he wonders if LeVar Burton, *Reading Rainbow*'s host, could enter it. "These are great ideas!" says Jill, the senior producer. "Now, let's go check them out!"

Helena and Marc, the researchers, investigate all the ideas. They contact experts, gather information, and double-check facts. Then they *survey*, or look for locations where *Reading Rainbow* can shoot the scenes. For *Always My Dad*, Central Park is chosen as a location. For three months, the staff prepares to videotape the "Family Day" race.

Meanwhile, Lee, the writer, toils over the script. She imagines the scenes in her head and writes them down. She reads the script out loud, to see if LeVar's lines sound natural. Sometimes she rewrites the script six or seven times until it's just right.

One month after all the research and planning are done, the *Reading Rainbow* crew arrives in Central Park at 6 o'clock in the morning to set up for the *Always My Dad* shoot. Today, LeVar will videotape the *wraps*, or wraparound segments, which are his special part of the show. In the wraps, LeVar talks about the theme of the show, and introduces the book and the other segments. It will take two hours to set up the lights and video camera for LeVar's wraps.

Ed, the director, plans how to shoot each scene. He frames the location with his hands, searching for the best angles to shoot the action.

Kevin, the director of photography, positions the lights so they'll shine on LeVar without casting shadows.

The sound engineer, Gary, attaches a microphone to the end of a long pole, or *boom*, which he'll hold over LeVar's head to record his voice. "Testing, one, two," Gary says, checking the volume.

On the other side of the set, the crew prepares for a moving, or *dolly*, shot. They lay 16 feet of steel track on the ground and put wooden blocks under the rungs to make the track level. Even though the ground is bumpy and uneven, the camera will move smoothly on the track as it follows LeVar.

At 7 o'clock, LeVar arrives on the set. Everyone's thrilled to see him! After working together for 12 years, he and the staff are like family. Before getting down to business, he greets the crew and the other actors. Then he discusses the script with the producer, makes a few changes, and learns his new lines. Randy, the makeup artist, dabs makeup on LeVar's face, so he'll look natural under the harsh bright lights. LeVar rehearses the scene a few times; then he's ready to roll.

"Quiet on the set!" yells Ari, the assistant director. "Action!" calls Ed.

The first few *takes*, or attempts, are a little rough. Once, LeVar forgets what he's supposed to say! Another time, the camera doesn't move fast enough to follow him. Finally, on the fifth take, everything works perfectly. The director shouts "Cut! That's a buy!" which means "Stop! That's a great take!" Everyone applauds, including bystanders who stopped to watch.

The *Reading Rainbow* crew spends all day in the park videotaping LeVar's wraps, breaking only once, to eat lunch.

Now that LeVar's wraps have been videotaped, it's time to produce all the other segments. The first is the book *adaptation*, the segment in which the book appears on the show.

Ronnie, the producer of this segment, gets the book ready to be filmed by a special camera. She thinks about how a child looking at the book would move his or her eyes around the page. Then, using *frames* that are the shape of a television screen, she makes a *storyboard*, or map of the story. A camera will then take pictures of the book, using the storyboard as its guide.

Before the pictures are shot, an actress, Broadway star B. J. Crosby, reads *Always My Dad* into a microphone. Her recorded voice will be combined with the book's pictures to create the adaptation.

A month later, the staff videotapes the *field segment*, or on-location adventure based on the theme of the book. Past field segments have featured erupting volcanos, Olympic skaters, migrating butterflies, tightrope walkers, Native American powwows, snakes, and dinosaur hunters—just to name a few. To tape these segments, LeVar and the crew have traveled around the world, from Maine to Mexico.

For *Always My Dad*, the field segment is a *documentary*, or real-life look at the Davis family. The crew follows the Davis family around with a camera and records a typical day in their lives.

It's hard for the Davis family to have a typical day when there's a camera pointed at them! But after a while they get used to the camera, and the crew tapes them shopping at the supermarket.

"La, la, lalala la . . ." Steve, the music director, composes a song for *Always My Dad*. The song will appear as a segment in the show, along with videotaped pictures that highlight the show's theme. Last night Steve read the *Always My Dad* script and fell asleep thinking about it, and this morning he jotted down notes on a napkin.

Now he's in the studio, developing the melody and lyrics with his writing partner, Janet.

Music is very important to television; no *Reading Rainbow* show goes on the air without it. In addition to writing songs, Steve also creates music for other parts of the show, like the book adaptation and the field segment.

Finally, after eight months, there's only one segment left to produce—the book reviews. The children who star in the book reviews aren't professional actors; they're just enthusiastic readers who live near New York City and try out when *Reading Rainbow* holds auditions at their schools.

When the kids arrive at the television studio, they're matched up with a book. They read it, decide what to say, and get ready to go on camera.

Randy, the makeup artist, brushes Amanda's hair.

Stacey and Robin, the book-review producers, help Naren rehearse. The big blue wall behind Naren will be replaced with a picture of the book he is reviewing by a special-effects machine called an *Ultimatte*.

At last, all the different pieces of the *Always My Dad* show have been taped. But they're still just pieces—someone has to put them together!

That job belongs to the editor. Tony uses computerized editing machines to fit the pieces together like a puzzle. For weeks Ed works with Tony to choose the best takes. They select wide shots and closeups, arrange them in the right order, and decide when to *cut away*, or go to the next shot. They put the scenes together so the show makes sense and the pace keeps moving.

Tony usually starts with 40 or 50 tapes. He edits and edits—until there's just one.

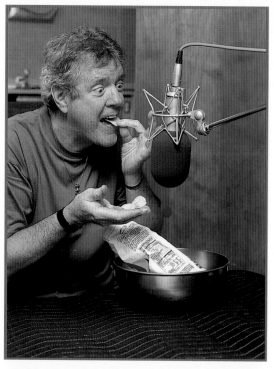

"Screech!" "Slurp!" "Slam!" Here come the sound effects that Lee, the post-production audio engineer, adds to *Reading Rainbow* shows to make them sound real.

Lee has over 30,000 different sounds on CDs. But if Lee can't find a sound on a CD, he makes it himself—crunching potato chips, tinkling bells—by doing whatever is necessary to create it.

Lee decides where to put sound effects into the edited tape of *Always My Dad*. Using a computer, he electronically places the sounds in exactly the right spots.

Lastly, Lee *mixes* the show, so the sound effects and music are loud and soft where they ought to be.

After ten months, *Always My Dad* is finished. At least 30 people have worked hard to create this show. Their goal was to make a show that children would enjoy—and they hope they've accomplished it!

Of course, the real test will come when *Always My Dad* goes on the air and millions of kids watch it. But the people who make *Reading Rainbow* won't tune in that day. They'll be hard at work, on location or in the studio, producing the next episode of *Reading Rainbow*.

For Paul, Eric, Brett,
and everyone at Reading Rainbow.

For Patty.

— R. K.

— C. H.

READING RAINBOW is a production of GPN/Nebraska ETV Network and WNED-TV, Buffalo, and is produced by Lancit Media Productions, Ltd., New York City.

READING RAINBOW© is a registered trademark of GPN/WNED-TV. For information and videocassettes, call GPN at 800-228-4630. For information on song CDs, tapes, and sheet music, contact Oasis Music, Inc., at 800-811-7210.

The "Reading Rainbow Theme Song" by Steve Horelick, Janet Weir, and Dennis Kleinman is reprinted on the book jacket and excerpted for the title of the book by permission of SCH Music, Inc. Copyright © 1981 by SCH Music, Inc. All rights reserved.

Material from *Always My Dad* by Sharon Dennis Wyeth and illustrated by Raúl Colón is reprinted by permission of Alfred A. Knopf, Inc. Copyright © 1994 by Sharon Dennis Wyeth and Raúl Colón.

Text copyright © 1997 by Ronnie Krauss
Photographs copyright © 1997 by Christopher Hornsby

First published in the United States of America in 1997 by Walker Publishing Company, Inc.

Published simultaneously in Canada by Thomas Allen & Son Canada, Limited, Markham, Ontario

Library of Congress Cataloging-in-Publication Data
Krauss, Ronnie.
   Take a look, it's in a book : how television is made at *Reading Rainbow*/
Ronnie Krauss ; photographs by Christopher Hornsby.
   p.   cm.
   Summary: Describes the television program "Reading Rainbow" and how it is made, from the selection of books featured to the addition of sound effects and music after shooting has been completed.
   ISBN 0-8027-8488-7. —ISBN 0-8027-8489-5 (reinforced)
   1. Reading Rainbow (Television program)—Juvenile Literature.
[1. Reading Rainbow (Television program) 2. Television—Production and direction.] I. Hornsby, Christopher. II. Title.
PN1992.77.R39K73 1997
791.45'72—dc20.
96-25984
CIP AC

Book design by Diane Stevenson of Snap-Haus Graphics

Printed in Hong Kong

10 9 8 7 6 5 4 3 2

Index

Date Due

DEC - 1 74						